ELECTION NIGHT

ELECTION NIGHT

Thomas R. Raber

Lerner Publications Company
Minneapolis

Acknowledgements

The illustrations are reproduced through the courtesy of: Dwight D. Eisenhower Library, pp. 2, 23; National Archives, pp. 6, 31, 66, 74 (top), 82; Courtesy of The New-York Historical Society, New York City, p. 7; AP/Wide World Photos, p. 9; Pictorial Parade, p. 10; Minnesota Historical Society, pp. 11, 16, 34, 52, 72 (bottom); Office of the Architect of the Capitol, p. 12; Office of the Speaker of the House, p. 13; Michael Evans/The White House, p. 14 (top); Mike Dukakis for President, p. 14 (bottom); Library of Congress, pp. 19 (bottom), 20, 24, 28 (right), 29, 30, 37, 38, 39, 48, 63, 68, 72 (top), 73, 77 (both); United Nations/Y. Nagata, p. 19 (top); Rutherford B. Hayes Library, p. 21; Courtesy, Museum of Fine Arts, Boston, p. 28 (left); Minnesota DFL Party, pp. 32, 85; N.A.A.C.P., pp. 41, 42, 43, 61, 70; Cleveland Public Library, p. 45; Smithsonian Institution, p. 52 (left); Dictionary of American Portraits, p. 54 (top); Independent Picture Service, p. 54 (bottom); U.S. Army Photograph, p. 55; U. S. Information Agency, National Archives, p. 56; Gerald R. Ford Library, pp. 57, 78; Minnesota *Daily*/Beddow, p. 59; Religious News Service, p. 65; St. Paul *Dispatch*, p. 74 (bottom); United Press International, p. 80; Minneapolis *Tribune*, p. 81.

Front cover photograph: Cindy Charles/Gamma-Liaison
Back cover photograph: Minnesota DFL Party

Cover illustration by Stephen Clement

The photo on page two shows Dwight D. Eisenhower celebrating his election to the presidency in 1956.

Library of Congress Cataloging-in-Publication Data

Raber, Thomas R.
    Election night/Thomas R. Raber.
      p. cm.
    Bibliography: p.
    Includes index.
    Summary: Describes elections and how they work in the United States.
    ISBN 0-8225-1751-5 (lib. bdg.)
    1. Elections—United States—Juvenile literature. [1. Elections. 2. Politics, Practical.] I. Title.
JK1978. R33 1988
324.973—dc19   88-22666
                                        CIP
                                        AC

Manufactured in the United States of America

1 2 3 4 5 6 7 8 9 97 96 95 94 93 92 91 90 89 88

Contents

Harry S Truman sits at his desk in the White House.

1
Election Night

At eight o'clock on election night 1948, President Harry S Truman looked like a sure loser. Rival candidate Thomas E. Dewey had taken an early lead, just as nearly everyone expected. And Truman—whom many did not consider a "real" president because he had not been elected but had taken office on the death of President Franklin D. Roosevelt—seemed certain to be sent packing from the White House.

Just before the election, a final **poll**, or prediction of the voters' support, showed Dewey likely to capture 49.5 percent of the vote to 44.5 percent for Truman. Many thought those results underestimated Dewey's strength. Since the summer, Dewey had seemed to be so far in

The New York Times *said before the election that "Thomas E. Dewey's election as President is a foregone conclusion."*

7

front that he was advised not to campaign too diligently. Why run an aggressive race against an underdog such as Truman and risk making a mistake that could erode his lead?

The public was upset with Truman for many reasons in 1948. One of the major reasons was his handling of the economic inflation that had gripped the country since the end of World War II. Inflation is a situation in which prices rise continuously. It becomes a bad situation when prices rise much faster than workers' pay does. The workers find it more difficult to afford items they could buy in the past. Truman's critics put a twist on something Herbert Hoover had said when Hoover successfully ran for president in 1928. Hoover had promised voters "A chicken in every pot, and a car in every garage." Truman's critics said "Truman" stood for, "Two families in every garage," and joked that "To err, is Truman."

Even Truman's own political party, the Democrats, deserted him. A political **party** is a group of people organized together to try to direct what the government does, and the Democratic Party is one such group. Candidates of the same party running for lesser offices usually like to be associated with the president.

They believe voters will think of them as more powerful politicians if they are seen being friendly with the president. But in the 1946 Congressional elections, many Democratic candidates had asked Truman to stay away from their campaigns because they did not want to be identified with him.

In 1948, two other candidates were expected to attract many Democratic voters. Henry Wallace, who had been a vice president under Roosevelt, was running as a Progressive Party candidate. At the same time, Strom Thurmond, the Democratic governor of South Carolina, was running as a States' Rights Democrat Party candidate. Thurmond's followers were known informally as the "Dixiecrats."

Truman even had trouble finding someone to run with him for vice president that year. He finally came up with 70-year-old Alben Barkley.

Old political wisdom says that public opinion doesn't shift much between early September and the election unless one candidate makes a serious error. Dewey had made none. Several national magazines even printed future issues referring to Dewey as "President Dewey," and his **running mate**, California Governor Earl Warren as "Vice President Warren."

Truman, however, did not believe he was going to lose. He ignored the experts and took his campaign directly to the people. Traveling by train, Truman conducted a "whistle stop" campaign, stopping at each little town on the train route to deliver a speech from the back platform of the last car.

Truman was well known for his plain speaking, and he used that trait effectively. Sometimes he began his address with the statement, "My name is Harry Truman. I work for the government. And I'd like to keep my job."

Truman spoke less like a world leader than like a common citizen, and people responded to his no-nonsense style. By election night Truman had covered 31,700 miles and averaged about 10 speeches a day. It is estimated that about 15,000,000 Americans heard him speak that fall.

Still, few people would have believed an upset was brewing.

"At six o'clock I was defeated," Truman recalled later. "At ten o'clock I was defeated. Twelve o'clock I was defeated. Four o'clock I had won the election. And the next morning

In his last whistle-stop speech, Truman said, "The smart boys say we couldn't win...but we called their bluff, we told the people the truth... All over the country I have seen it in the people's faces. The people are going to win this election."

...I was handed this paper which said, 'Dewey Defeats Truman.'"

Historians explain that Dewey made a mistake by campaigning so sparingly. He avoided talking about important issues and did not offer solutions to them. He looked indecisive and vague to many voters. Unlike Truman, he seemed stuffy and "above" the people.

Truman's victory showed the power of an **incumbent** president to win votes. An incumbent is one who is currently in office. Even if an incumbent is unpopular, he or she is still familiar to the voters. And voters often like to stick with candidates who are known to them.

Yet, Truman also proved the need for an incumbent to get out and campaign. No matter how well known a president's personality and views may be, he or she must travel the country to express his or her ideas to voters.

Truman's surprise victory of 1948 is remembered as one of the closest elections in history. It is also remembered as one of the most exciting elections in history. It is a good example of what can happen on election night.

2

Election Scope

What voters decide on election night is far more than merely who will become president. Most elections, in fact, do not include a presidential race. A presidential election occurs only once every four years, but federal elections, in which United States senators and representatives are chosen, take place every two years. Other important elections occur even more often.

A state or a smaller community may hold some type of election every year—maybe more than once a year—to choose persons for various small and large offices. In any given election, a voter might be asked to choose his or her favorite for **federal**, or national, offices such as U.S. senator and U.S. representative; state offices such as governor, lieutenant governor, state legislator, treasurer, or auditor; and city or county offices such as mayor, sheriff, prosecutor, judge, council member, or school board member.

VOTE FOR THESE
FARMER-LABOR CANDIDATES
———
Henrik Shipstead . . .   U. S. Senator
Magnus Johnson . . . . Governor
Arthur A. Siegler . . Lieut. Governor
Susie W. Stageberg.. . Sec'y of State
Frank H. Keyes . . . . . . Treasurer
Eliza Evans Deming . . . . Auditor
Roy C. Smelker . . Attorney General
H. T. Van Lear Clerk Supreme Court
W. W. Royster R. R. and Warehouse Comm.
W. A. Anderson Judge Supreme Court
(No Party Designation—Farmer-Labor Endorsed)

This includes a candidate for "Railroad and Warehouse Commissioner."

The voter might also be asked to decide on proposals to raise taxes, or on proposals called referenda or initiatives. These are proposals to approve or repeal laws and they are voted on directly by the people, by-passing the usual legislative process.

Here are the larger offices and issues that might be decided on election night.

United States Senator

The U.S. Congress is made up of both the Senate and House of Representatives. The U.S. Senate was created as part of the "Great Compromise." At the Constitutional Convention of 1787, prominent people from each state got together to write a new Constitution. The United States had been a country since the Articles of Confederation were written in 1781, but the Articles had not worked very well. Now they had decided to fine-tune the government which made up the United States of America.

One of the major problems the writers of the Constitution faced was how states should be represented in the national government. States with small populations preferred that every state send an equal

At the Constitutional Convention in 1787, the delegates met to revise the Articles of Confederation but ended up writing an entirely new document and setting up a new form of government.

number of representatives to the national congress. States with large populations, however, felt they deserved an advantage in the national government because of their size.

In the Great Compromise, the national government was made up of two law-making groups. The House of Representatives gives states representation based on their size. Therefore more-populous states have more votes in the House. The Senate gives equal representation to all states. The small states have as many votes as the big ones.

Each state elects two senators, making a total of 100 in office. Every senator is elected for six years, but the terms are staggered so that they do not all end at once. Roughly one-third come up for reelection every two years.

Senators originally were chosen by each state's legislators, but the 17th Amendment to the Constitution, made law in 1913, changed the system. Senators now are chosen by **popular vote** or the vote of the people. Each Senator represents all of the people in the state.

The Constitution requires that a candidate for senator be at least 30 years old, a citizen of the United States for 9 years, and a resident of the state he or she hopes to represent.

United States Representative

All 50 states have equal power in the Senate. But it is different in the House of Representatives. There the state of New York, for example, outnumbers South Dakota 34 representatives to 1.

In all, there are over 400 members of the House, and each serves a two-year term. That means a lot of power can change hands on one election night, and then again just two years later. On the average, 15

Thomas P. (Tip) O'Neill, a Massachusetts Democrat, was Speaker of the House of Representatives from 1977 until 1987. The Speaker is the leader of the House.

13

to 20 percent of the seats will change representatives in any one election. The record turnover was in 1894 when the Republican party increased the number of its representatives in the House by 120.

Representatives are elected by the voters in a certain **district** or portion of a state. They are supposed to act for the voters who live in the area which makes up their district.

The Constitution says a candidate for the House must be at least 25 years old, a citizen of the United States for at least 7 years, and a resident of the state in which he or she runs.

Governor

Governors generally serve four years and their term usually ends in a non-presidential election year. States vary in the number of re-elections they may allow a governor.

In 1789, only New York, Massachussets, Rhode Island, Connecticut, and Vermont elected their governors by popular vote. The other original eight states had their state legislatures choose a governor. By the 1860s, however, those 8 states had switched to the popular vote and each new state after the original 13, with the exception of Louisiana,

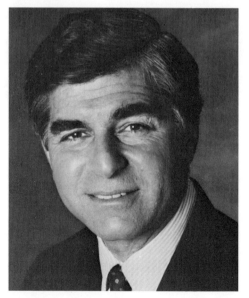

Ronald Reagan (above) and Michael Dukakis (below) both served as governors before launching presidential campaigns.

14

came into being using the popular vote. Today, all states use the popular vote when electing a governor.

It is common in some states for many candidates to run for governor. If one candidate does not win more than 50 percent of the vote, some states require that the election be decided in the state legislature. Other states allow the public to vote again, choosing between the top two candidates, in a **runoff election**.

Direct Legislation Proposals

Along with the choices for political office there also may be on a ballot items of **direct legislation**. These are laws that bypass the usual lawmaking procedure, or laws that need approval by the voters.

Direct legislation proposals come in two basic types:

Initiatives, in which people write proposed laws. If a certain number of voters sign a petition favoring a proposed law, the proposal must be voted on either by the voters or by the lawmaking body.

Referenda, in which laws already passed by the legislature, or even some kinds of laws that only have been proposed by the legislature, are put on a ballot for the people to vote on.

Some proposals are for ordinary statutes, others are for amendments or changes in the state's constitution. Most states require that all constitutional amendments be voted on by the people after they are passed by the legislature.

All initiatives, and some referenda, are started by people submitting petitions, or lists of signatures, to the government. State laws normally require a lot of signatures. Statewide initiatives usually require about eight percent of the number of votes cast for governor in the last general election to be placed on a ballot. Statewide referenda need about four percent of the same figure.

In addition to state proposals, there may be local or community initiatives on the ballot that are up for approval after having met similar petition requirements.

Off-year or Midterm Elections

Elections held in non-presidential years are known as **off-year** or **midterm** elections and they are notable for two reasons.

First, the political party that won the presidency usually loses seats in Congress to the opposing party in the midterm election. By voting against the party in power, people may be sending a message to the president's party not to become too confident.

Second, a much smaller number of voters participate in off-year elections than in presidential elections. People presumably do not consider midterm elections as important or as glamorous as presidential elections.

In races for offices other than president, the public usually bases its decisions on much less information about the candidates. Candidates for lower offices spend less money on the campaigns, and they have less chance to make themselves widely recognized. Because the voters may know so little about the candidates and the issues, they may base their decisions on easy clues about the candidates. For example: Is the candidate an incumbent? Is he or she a Democrat or a Republican? Where does he or she stand on the one issue that most matters to the individual voter?

A postcard advertising the Farmer-Labor Party's candidates for office about 1926

3

Candidates and Strategies

Running for political office takes more than knowledge about government. A candidate at any level must have ambition, organization, and money on his or her side.

Both political parties conduct seminars for potential candidates to teach them every aspect of running a campaign. A candidate's job experience, family background, race, religion, party, and strategy are the elements that may influence the election's result.

Though there is no single background that best prepares a candidate for politics, there are patterns to be found in the experiences of those who enter the field.

By far, most people who run for office have studied law. In the U.S.

Congress in 1985, two-thirds of the senators and more than half of the representatives were certified lawyers. Few factory workers, construction workers, scientists, doctors, or teachers make it into national politics, although some are elected to local offices.

There are several reasons for this. Much of government is about the law and legality. Lawyers are experienced in the art of persuasion, which is a key to effective politics. A lawyer also works with or works for businesspeople who can help a political career with money and influential contacts.

Most candidates for national offices are white males. Of the 535 members of the U.S. Senate and

House in 1985, for example, 24 were women, 20 were black, and a few were of Hispanic, Asian, or Middle Eastern origins. The Constitution reflected the views of the 1770s that neither minorities nor women were able to make political decisions. These groups have only slowly gained the right to vote and to participate in politics.

The largest single religious group in the United States is Protestant Christian, and the candidates who are successful in gaining office reflect the voters' beliefs. About three-fourths of the members of the 1985 Congress were Protestant Christians.

Women Candidates

Women candidates have been more successful in recent elections than they were in the country's early history. There are now women serving in political offices from school board all the way up to U.S. senator.

In 1916, Republican Jeannette Rankin of Montana was elected to the U.S. House of Representatives. She became the country's first congresswoman four years before women could vote. She served one term and retired, then ran again and was elected in 1940.

In 1922, Democrat Rebecca Felton became the first woman U.S. senator. Felton was appointed by the governor of Georgia to succeed a senator who had died during his term. She served until a specially scheduled election produced a new senator. In 1932, Democrat Hattie Caraway of Arkansas became the first woman elected a senator in her own right.

No woman has yet come close to being elected president, but in 1984, a woman finally became a vice presidential candidate for one of the two major parties. U.S. Representative Geraldine Ferraro of New York ran as the vice presidential candidate of the Democratic party.

Black Candidates

Although black people won the right to vote before women did, it has taken longer for them to gain and keep influence in politics. Black people were freed in 1863 and were guaranteed the right to vote by Constitutional amendment after the Civil War. Several black candidates quickly won political office. But white politicians soon passed laws limiting those voting rights. The fortunes of black candidates turned poor and remained that way for decades.

In recent years, black candidates have met with somewhat greater success. The most visible accomplishments have been made by Jesse Jackson. He won two presidential **primary** elections during the 1984 campaign and won 10 percent of the vote in several other primaries. Primary elections help the parties select the person who will represent

Below: The first black senator and representatives were elected to Congress in 1869, all from southern states.
Right: Andrew Young of Georgia was elected to the U. S. House of Representatives in 1972. He was the first black elected to Congress from the South since 1901.

their party in the national election for the presidency. In 1988, Jackson was again a contender to become the Democratic candidate.

The Power of Incumbency

In the United States House and Senate, incumbents of each party have success rates of 80 to 90 percent. That is, incumbents who decide to run again will win 80 to 90 times out of 100 races. In 1980, for example, 392 incumbents ran and 360 (92 percent) were reelected. For incumbent governors the success rate is about 60 percent.

Incumbents have several advantages over other candidates: first, their campaign staff, organization, funding, and strategy have already proved successful and the framework is already in place to reach the voters again. Second, incumbents usually are better known than their opponents because they have served in office and can claim credit for what the government accomplished while they served. Third, incumbents in some offices are allowed to mail information to their constituents for free, and they may be given an allowance to travel on business throughout their districts. Although these allowances are supposed to be used to serve the public and not for campaigning, it is often impossible to separate these goals.

The most common reason an incumbent is *not* reelected is that he or she has made a serious error in office. In 1980, for example, five Congressional Democrats were caught in a scandal. The Federal

In this cartoon, Uncle Sam is saying "After all is said and done, he's still 'Good Enough for Me.'" Theodore Roosevelt was easily reelected in 1904.

20

Bureau of Investigation (FBI) allegedly offered certain representatives bribes, asking for legislative favors in return. The FBI was checking rumors that some legislators could be paid to change their votes on issues. These five Democrats accepted the FBI's money. Four of the five were defeated in the next election.

Party Identification

Some people vote by "brand names." In political terms, this means they vote by political parties. These voters trust the label "Republican" or "Democrat," even if they are not familiar with the individual candidates on the ballot. Most American voters describe themselves as either Democrats or Republicans, even though relatively few people are active members of either party.

Political parties used to hold more power. In 1920, for example, voters in only 3.2 percent of all the nation's Congressional districts **split their tickets** supporting one party for president and the other for a Congressional seat. (A **ticket** in an election is the list of candidates sponsored by one party.) Most of the voters in 1920 supported a

straight ticket. But by the 1960s, about 15 percent of the electorate were regularly splitting their tickets, and by 1980 more than half split their tickets.

Political parties can still mean a great deal to the candidates, however. Most candidates for political office must go through one round of

A Republican voter advertised his strong belief in Rutherford B. Hayes as a candidate in the presidential 1876 election.

21

elections to win the party's support before they run in the "real" election for the office. The **primary** election, usually held months before the general election, is the party election. It is held to select who will run for the party in the general election. A candidate's opponents in a primary are members of his or her own party, and in some states voters must vote a straight party ticket in a primary. That is, a registered Republican can only choose among Republican candidates. He or she cannot vote for or against a Democrat in a primary. The winner of the primary gains the help of the party in the form of money, "brand name," and advice. This direct competition among political "allies" can make primary races for the party nomination as intense as those for the office itself.

Filing First

Long before election night, people who plan to run for any office must file as candidates. That means they must fill out a form, and maybe pay a fee, at the appropriate government office of the community, saying they want to become a candidate.

It is an advantage to be first on the ballot, since lazy voters may not read to the bottom of the list of candidates. The first spot on the ballot usually is given to the candidate who is first to register unless the election rules call for alphabetical order. So, long before the election, some candidates or their supporters will camp outside the election offices in order to be first to register. Each state or county has different deadlines, but usually a candidate must file about two months before the primary date.

Party Strategy

In any election, leaders of each party do their homework, devising detailed plans to win as many Congressional seats as possible. Local chapters of each party may mobilize behind candidates for local offices, but the national party's attention is given to the big elections: Congress and the presidency. The more seats a party controls in Congress, the more votes the party can muster for its goals and programs when Congress is in session.

When plotting strategy, campaigners classify Congressional districts as one of three types:
♦ A **swing** district is one that has been won by a Republican *and*

by a Democrat in recent elections. It might "swing" to either party in the next election.

♦ A **marginal** district is one in which recent elections have been won or lost by no more than 5 percent of the vote. No lead is safe there.

♦ A **target** district is one that an opposing party thinks it has a good chance to take over. The party will spend a lot of effort trying to win a target district. Often marginal districts are also classified as targets.

Presidential Coattails

In 1964, President Lyndon Johnson defeated Republican Senator Barry Goldwater by a huge margin. Johnson's fellow Democrats gained 37 seats in the House of Representatives. Some political experts called this double good fortune an example of presidential "coattails" working for the Democrats. The coattail belief is an old campaign idea that candidates for other offices from the same party can benefit from the success of a popular presidential candidate. Some experts believe that the presidential candidate's popularity can affect elections all the way down to mayor or judge. The

Dwight Eisenhower (left) with Soviet Premier Nikita Khrushchev. Eisenhower was a popular president, but this did not carry over to help other Republicans running in 1956.

fellow candidates are said to be swept into office by riding the successful presidential candidate's coattails.

Although there is some truth to the explanation, it does not always hold true. In 1956, for instance, popular President Dwight Eisenhower ran a strong campaign, but his fellow Republicans lost two seats in the House.

23

In spite of George Washington's fear and dislike of political parties, the Republican Party has often claimed Washington as its founder. This campaign banner from 1888 shows the spirits of (left to right) Abraham Lincoln, Ulysses S. Grant, Washington, Chester A. Arthur, and James A. Garfield hovering over the Republican candidates.

4
Political Parties

In his farewell to the presidency, George Washington warned the nation about the evils of political parties. He said he dreaded the thought of "two great parties, each under its own leader" acting as a threat to democracy.

Yet even when he was president, Washington was generally regarded as a member of the Federalist Party. And even as he made his farewell address, a two-party system was developing in the United States.

Originally, American politicians and voters avoided becoming formally organized. When the United States government was being created, no one was certain of its future. The politicians were reluctant to divide themselves into parties. They feared that parties would split the country and make it impossible for the government to function. They feared parties might bring the new nation down. But as the country headed into the 1800s, with several elections under its belt, people began to see a need to unite with those who thought like they did. Political allies could help them make their points of view into laws.

The Need for Parties

Political parties may serve several functions in government:
- They give voters who have not studied the issues or the candidates at least one reason for their voting decision. Lazy voters can

vote on the basis of party philosophy or party name.

♦ They stimulate competition among politicians. The party out of power serves as watchdog over the party in office.

♦ They provide a structure that keeps the government running in an orderly way between elections.

♦ They create a sense of cooperation and duty among officials of the same party. This may help the politicians to get things done. However, if this "team spirit" makes politicians of different parties unwilling to cooperate with each other, it can keep government from acting effectively.

♦ Candidates may find that their first need is the approval of party members. Parties may help discourage unqualified candidates from seeking office.

♦ Parties help raise funds for campaigns.

What the Parties Stand For

Very little can be said about either of the two major parties in the United States—or any other parties anywhere— that is absolutely always true. Both the Republican and the Democratic Party are made up of individuals. There is much overlap and duplication, as well as difference, in the way these individuals view politics.

It is impossible to list the point of view of each party completely, because that point of view varies so much from individual to individual and from month to month. A general outline of the beliefs of the two major parties might be helpful, however.

The Republicans In general, Republicans believe:

♦ The power of the national government should be limited as much as possible. State and local governments, which are closer to the people, should be allowed to provide more immediate service.

♦ Government itself should be kept small. Its purpose is not to control people with regulations, but simply to provide what people cannot provide for themselves.

♦ Private business should be allowed to prosper independently. Governments should regulate or control businesses no more than necessary to protect the public interest.

♦ Helping businesses succeed helps the poor get jobs more

effectively than giving money or aid directly to the poor.

♦ Determined, independent people can shape their own futures without government help or interference.

The Democrats   In general, Democrats believe:

♦ A strong national government is needed to deal with modern problems because many problems are too complex and costly to be solved by state or local governments.

♦ The federal government should intervene in the affairs of business when its intervention is needed to keep the economy strong.

♦ The federal government should provide social services to needy citizens. These services might include low-cost health care for the elderly, low-cost housing for the poor, job training for the unemployed, or loans to students who want to attend college.

In recent history, Democrats have been widely supported by minorities and the poor. Republican candidates have often been supported by voters in business.

Democrats traditionally accuse Republicans of siding with big companies against the interest of workers. Republicans accuse Democrats of squandering the taxpayers' money on social programs—like health care—which cost too much and help too few.

In recent years, however, the parties have been acting more like each other. Some Republicans have suggested spending more and expanding the federal government's role; some Democrats have suggested spending less and reducing the federal government's role. The distinction between the parties is becoming so blurred that today many people believe there is no real difference between them.

Why Only Two Parties?

The Federalists were a strong party in the early 1800s. The Whigs became strong a little later. Although both disbanded long ago, in their times they were every bit as influential as the Democratic and Republican parties are now. That is because each existed as one of *two* major parties of the day.

The United States has always functioned under a **two-party system**. Although more than two parties may struggle for influence, the power has

Thomas Jefferson (left) and his friends gave rise to the Democratic-Republicans, and Alexander Hamilton (right) and his friends founded the Federalists.

continually swung back and forth between two main rivals.

One of the reasons the two-party system took hold in this country is that party politics in the United States began as a two-way struggle. Originally, the Federalists formed in favor of a strong central government, and the Democratic-Republicans organized as their opposition.

But the big reason the United States has a two-party system is because the United States has **winner-take-all** elections. In Congressional elections, for example, the candidate who collects the most votes wins the position as district representative. All other candidates lose.

But in countries where systems such as **proportional representation** are used, seats may be won according to the percentage of the votes each party receives. A party that wins 20 percent of the vote would send 20 percent of the representatives to the legislature. Such a system encourages candidates from minority parties to run even if they know they cannot get more votes than their opponents. At least they can win a toe-hold of influence and hope to increase it in future elections.

The winner-take-all system makes

it difficult for minority parties to gain power. Voters are reluctant to "waste" their votes on small-party candidates when they believe a major-party candidate will win. If a candidate cannot win a majority, he or she has little to gain by running.

Third Parties

In the 1850s, a group called the Native American Party or "The Order of the Star Spangled Banner" sprang up, rallying behind the slogan "Purify the Ballot Box." They operated like a secret society, working undercover. Their goals were to stop immigrants from coming into the country and to keep anyone who was born in a foreign country from holding office. If any of the party members were asked about their activities, they were sworn to reply "I know nothing." This gave them the nickname the "Know-Nothings."

At their peak, the Know-Nothings elected 8 of the country's 62 U.S. senators and 104 of the 234 U.S. representatives of the time. In 1856, they ran a candidate in the presidential race, Millard Fillmore. Fillmore won only in the state of Maryland, however, and when the Civil War began the party went into decline. But the Know-Nothings remain an example of what is known as a **third party**—an alternative to the two major parties currently on the scene.

Third parties often have been formed around a single major issue, such as "law and order." In 1875, for example, the Greenback Party sought help for farmers who were deeply in debt. They were called Greenbackers because they believed the farmers' financial problems could be solved if the government

Millard Fillmore, former president, was neither a Know-Nothing nor a believer in the party's goals, but the party chose him as its candidate in 1856 anyway.

would print more dollars. In 1878, the Greenbackers elected 14 members to the U.S. Congress, but the party soon fell off in popularity.

Some third parties are not formed to support a particular cause but instead split from one of the major parties. These new parties attract those unhappy with the ideas of the major parties. In 1912, Republican Theodore Roosevelt disagreed with his party's candidate and launched his own presidential campaign as a Progressive Republican. His "Bull Moose" party (because Roosevelt said he felt "fit as a bull moose") attracted other Republicans who were dissatisfied with the Republican Party.

Third parties rarely win the presidency or a majority in any legislature. But third parties do not always enter a political race because they expect to win. Sometimes they use a campaign simply to publicize their cause and win new followers. Because they rarely control any major offices, they are not responsible for keeping the government working. This means they do not have to compromise with their opponents. They can keep their goals "pure." They can also hope that, in time, their popularity might force the major parties to accept their ideas and work toward some of their goals. Many widespread reforms in America began as the goals of third-party candidates— old-age pensions, public health programs, shorter work days, and prohibition, to name a few.

Theodore Roosevelt was a loyal Republican when he was William McKinley's running mate in 1900 and when he was elected president in 1904.

The "Spoiler" Role

Occasionally, third parties have contributed to the defeat of one the major parties. In 1844, for example, Liberty Party candidate James Birney received 2.3 percent of the popular vote, allowing James Polk to defeat Henry Clay 49.5 percent to 48.1 percent.

Third-party campaigns have only rarely decided a race, however. In 1948, the renegade States' Rights Democrats ("Dixiecrats") and Progressive Democrats both took Democratic voters away from Democrat Harry Truman, but they did not deny him victory.

Problems of Third Parties

In any election, third-party candidates are the underdogs. They are likely to be working with less money and fewer staff members than the major-party candidates. They also seem less prestigious, less trustworthy, and less familiar to the voters. Third parties are less likely to be featured in newspaper, radio, or television reports of the campaigns. In some communities, a third party faces stiff requirements to even qualify to put a candidate's name on the ballot. The party may have to get signatures from a number of people equal to five percent of the votes cast for a particular office in the last election.

In recent years, some of the most visible third parties have been the Socialist, the Socialist Labor, the

Norman Thomas (center, with fist up-raised) was the Socialist Party presidential candidate six times.

Socialist Workers, the Communist, and the Libertarian parties. These parties generally put up candidates for president and other national offices but receive only a trace of the vote.

Voters may be attracted to third parties, but their final choice is usually a Democrat or Republican. In 1980, early polls showed Independent candidate John Anderson was the choice of about 20 percent of the voters. Fewer than seven percent actually voted for him. His unsuccessful campaign is a good example of the strength of the two-party system in America. People may be unhappy with both major parties, but few care to use their vote for an alternative.

John F. Kennedy (without hat) won the presidency by a small margin of popular vote in 1960. But he won by a much bigger margin where it counts: in the electoral college.

5

The Electoral College

When Ronald Reagan won the presidency in 1980, he won only 51 percent of the nation's popular vote and his victory was called a "landslide." If the Philadelphia Phillies had won just 51 percent of their baseball games that season, their successful National League pennant drive would not have been called a "runaway."

Reagan's victory was decisive because of the total votes he won in what is known as the **electoral college system**. In electoral college votes, Reagan topped Jimmy Carter by a whopping 489 to 49, and Independent candidate John Anderson collected no electoral votes at all.

In the popular vote, most presidential elections are very close races.

Rarely does a winner receive more than 60 percent of the popular vote. But in presidential elections, popular votes are only secondarily important. The electoral votes are the crucial ones, and they made Reagan the big victor in 1980.

How the Electoral College Works

In voting for any other office, each vote counts directly for the candidate of the citizen's choice. But in a presidential and vice presidential election, a citizen's vote actually is cast for an **elector**—a person who, in turn, casts a vote for the presidential ticket.

Electors usually are influential party members who have been

33

A Democratic state convention in the 1930s. At state conventions, the active members of a party may choose the party's candidates or its electors.

nominated in primary elections or have been chosen at their party's state **convention**. A convention is a gathering of the party's members to decide on candidates and issues. The average voter may never see an elector or know any elector's name because in many states the electors are not named on the presidential ballot.

The electors promise to cast their vote for the candidate who wins the popular vote in their state, but the Constitution does not say they must. Sometimes a "faithless" elector casts a vote that does not reflect the wishes of his or her state's people.

The number of electors selected by each state is equal to the sum of its U.S. representatives and senators. Therefore, states with larger populations have more electoral votes. California and Illinois have many more votes than Delaware, Alaska, or Wyoming. People living in Washington, D.C.—which has no representatives or senators—could not vote in presidential elections until a law passed in 1961 awarded the district three electoral votes.

On election night, the candidate who **polls**, or receives from the voters, the largest number of popular votes in a particular state wins *all* of that state's electoral votes. And the winning candidate does not even need a majority (more than half) of the state's popular votes. He or she only needs to poll more votes than the opposition. This explains how candidates may be close in the popular vote, but still far apart in electoral votes. If a candidate wins the popular vote in Illinois, even by a slim margin, he or she gains 24 electoral votes. But a candidate who wins the popular vote in Delaware—even by a huge margin—captures only three electoral votes. The key to victory, therefore, is to win the big states. It takes a majority, 270 electoral votes, to win.

History of the System

The electoral college system was first used in 1789 in the United States' first presidential election. George Washington won 69 electoral votes, defeating John Adams. Adams, as was the custom at the time, earned the vice presidency by finishing second. Only 10 of the original 13 states participated.

The electoral college, which is outlined in Article II, Section 1 of the Constitution, came about as a compromise between lawmakers who wanted the president and vice president elected by direct popular vote and those who wanted them appointed by Congress or the state legislatures.

Small states feared that a system of direct popular vote would give populous states too much power over less populous states. Some of the Constitution's framers also feared that a direct popular vote would give too much power to common people, whom they did not trust to make good decisions. On the other hand, some of the framers feared that if Congress or the state legislatures chose the president, he or she would owe favors to politicians who did the choosing.

As an attempt to please everyone, the framers of the Constitution came up with the electoral college.

"Faithless Elector"

The men who wrote the Constitution intended the electors to be respected citizens who would weigh the vote of the people and use their own good judgment in casting their votes in the electoral college. It was understood that the electors were morally obligated to give great weight to the will of the people.

In some states today, electors are

obligated to vote as the public has voted, but in other states it is merely customary. In any case, the "faithless" elector—one who votes in opposition to the people's choice—is rare. In all the presidential elections, only 10 electors have not honored their pledge.

In 1968, for example, Virginia elector Roger Lea MacBride did not vote as pledged for President Richard Nixon and Vice President Spiro Agnew, calling them "crooks." Instead, he cast his vote for John Hospers and Theodora Nathan of the Libertarian Party.

According to law, Congress must respect the decisions of electors unless it believes an elector has been bribed. A statute passed in 1887 says the two houses of Congress may reject an elector's vote if they believe the vote was not "regularly given."

Winning More Votes and Losing

Another quirk in the electoral college system is that a candidate can win more popular votes than his or her opponents and still lose the election. It can happen when a candidate wins many big states by small margins while losing many little states by big margins.

In the election of 1888, Republican Benjamin Harrison won the presidency with 5,439,853 popular votes to Democrat Grover Cleveland's greater total of 5,540,309. Harrison captured the electoral college 233 to 168 amid charges that Republican politicians had bought the votes needed to win Indiana, a key state, and had bribed the corrupt Democrats of New York City to fix the New York State vote for Harrison.

With the election won, Harrison called his victory "providence." Others laughed, saying that "providence" had nothing to do with it.

A more common reason for a candidate to win an election with less than a majority of the popular vote is that the vote has been split among several candidates.

In all, 15 presidents have been elected with a **plurality**, or the greatest number of votes, rather than a majority, or more than half of the votes. Abraham Lincoln's three opponents in 1860 had a combined total 2,810,501 votes to Lincoln's 1,866,352, but because he had won more votes than any single opponent, he won the presidency.

Into the House

What if no candidate gets a majority of electoral votes? In 1824

Andrew Jackson earned more popular votes *and* more electoral votes than John Quincy Adams—but Adams wound up in the White House. Jackson lost because he could not win a majority in the electoral college over Adams and two other candidates.

If no candidate wins a majority in the electoral college, the Constitution says that the House of Representatives must select a president

President John Quincy Adams (right) gave a reception for Senator Andrew Jackson (center).

from the three candidates with the highest number of electoral votes. Each state is allowed one vote for president. The representatives from each state decide among themselves who will cast their state's vote.

Besides Adams, only Thomas Jefferson became president by a vote of the House. It happened in 1801 after the election of 1800 ended in confusion.

In those days, presidential and vice presidential candidates did not run as teams. Instead, *every* candidate ran for president. Whoever finished in second place became vice president.

In a race between two members of the Democratic-Republican Party, Jefferson and Aaron Burr both earned 73 electoral votes. The Democratic-Republican electors had caused the tie by accident. They had failed to withhold a vote for Burr, whom they intended to make vice president. The vote was thrown into the House to decide and a fierce struggle ensued. The election took 36 ballots to decide.

In the hope of preventing similar problems in the future, the 12th Amendment to the Constitution, ratified in 1804, provided that all votes be designated specifically for president or vice president. Soon after, presidential and vice presidential candidates began running as teams, as they do today, and a vote for president became a vote for the ticket as a whole.

When the President Becomes President

Although election night—the popular vote—is in November, the electors formally cast their ballots on the Monday following the second Wednesday in December in their respective state capitols.

The results are counted officially in the U.S. Capitol during the first week of January in the presence of the House and Senate. Only after the president of the Senate announces the count is the president of the United States officially elected.

A Final Note

In 1872, Republican President Ulysses Grant was reelected over Liberal Republican candidate Horace Greeley. Between election night and the meeting of the presidential electors, however, Greeley died, leaving the 66 electors he had won no one to vote for.

The electors' votes were split among various candidates, but three

Horace Greeley was a publisher and the founder and editor of the New York Tribune. *He was the 1872 presidential candidate of the Liberal Republicans and was supported by some Democrats.*

Georgia electors insisted on casting their votes for Greeley. Congress refused to count their votes, however, so it is official: no dead person has ever received an electoral vote for president.

6
At the Polls

While the rest of the nation sleeps, the people of Dixville Notch, New Hampshire, are casting their ballots. They have voted at midnight every election day for more than a century. In each election, Dixville Notch is the first polling place in the country to open, the first to close, and the first to report its tallies. That is partly because there is not a lot of counting to do. In 1984, Dixville Notch cast 29 votes for President Ronald Reagan and 1 for Walter Mondale.

Because elections are run by state and local governments, not the federal government, there is great variety in the way elections take place across the country. In some communities the **polls**, or places to

Women voting in Boston in 1888. Local laws allowed women to vote in some elections long before they had the right to vote in all elections.

39

vote, open at 6:00 A.M., and in others at 7:00 A.M. In some communities, the taverns may be ordered closed for election day, while in others a candidate might buy a round of beers at a bar near the polls while waiting for the polls to close.

Few rules apply to every community, so any discussion of the voting process must be full of the words "often," "sometimes," "frequently," and "commonly."

One condition is definite about any national general election: It takes place on a Tuesday early in November. Many people mistakenly believe it is always the first Tuesday of the month, but actually it is the first Tuesday after the first Monday in November.

Congress decided on that formula and passed it into law January 23, 1845. The formula combined a number of compromises. Monday was ruled out because in the 1800s many voters had to start for the polls the day before an election to make it on time, and many objected to traveling on Sunday. The first Tuesday in November was ruled out because it might fall on the first of the month and be inconvenient to people in business. The second Tuesday in November was eliminated because it might fall too close to the first Wednesday in December, which had already been set as the date the electoral college met to cast its ballots for president.

The current formula was the solution.

Registration

In order to be eligible to vote, a voter must be **registered**. All this means is that a voter must put his or her name onto the list of voters who vote in a particular district or precinct. The purpose of registration is to keep the voting process orderly and accurate. If a person tries to vote twice in an election, for example, the registration list helps authorities prevent the voter from doing so.

It is possible to register at many libraries, government buildings, and public schools, and at some shopping centers. Many states require prospective voters to register 30 days before the election in which they wish to vote, but in some others prospective voters may register at the polling place and vote on the spot.

To register, a prospective voter must show official proof that he or she will be 18 or older on election day and that he or she is a citizen

A young man and his pet in Baltimore, Maryland, remind voters to register.

vote in every general election. If a person's registration expires, he or she may simply renew it.

Some states may take away a citizen's right to vote if the person is convicted of certain crimes: most felonies, treason, or crimes relating to the electoral process. In some states, a voter would need a pardon from the governor to regain the right to vote. Other states may renew a person's right to vote when the person completes his or her sentence. Crimes related to the voting process, such as tampering with ballots to change the outcome of an election, may be treated as minor offenses and not require a jail term. These crimes, if minor, usually take away the criminal's right to vote for about three years.

Casting a Vote

Registered voters are notified by mail of all upcoming elections and where they should go to cast their votes. A polling place usually will be in a school, a church, a union hall, or some other public building in their **precinct**. A precinct is a political area set up for the purpose of collecting and counting the votes. It usually includes between 500 and 1,000 voters.

of the United States. A prospective voter may also need to prove that he or she has lived in the state for a certain period, usually 30 days.

Registration is usually permanent, but in some states voters will be taken off the rolls if they have not voted for a certain period of time. Some states require a voter to vote at least every few years to stay registered, others say the voter must

As voters approach the polling place they may be met by a crew of campaign workers, who urge them to vote for certain candidates. The campaign workers might hand the voters a list of names—like a shopping list—so the voters will remember who to vote for when they get into the building. Talking to voters just before they vote is called **election-eering**, and it is not allowed on the grounds of the polling place. The **electioneers**, or campaign workers, are required to stay a specified distance from the polling place door, usually about 100 feet.

In the polling place, voters will be asked to sign their names and give their addresses so an **election judge** can check to see if they are registered. There may be a long line of people waiting to vote, but voters need not worry. If a voter is in line at the time the polls close, he or she still will be allowed to vote.

Each voter goes into a booth which screens him or her from the view of other voters and of the election officials. Voters can take as long as they want to make their choices. They will either mark a paper ballot or, more likely, use a machine to record their choices. A voter marks the ballot and turns it in or flips a switch so that the

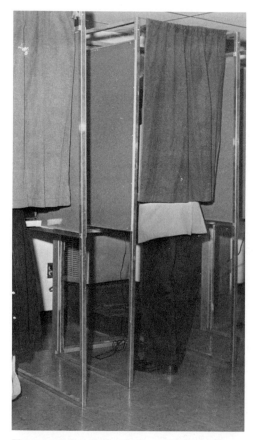

Voters make their choices in the privacy of a voting booth.

machine records the vote. That's all there is to it.

Election Officials

Election Judges   Election judges are the people who run the polls. Normally they are temporary city or county employees who are paid between $50 and $100 for their work on election day.

Most polling places are assigned four or more judges, who are divided equally between the two major parties. Although some judges may only work part of the day, the party representation at the polling place must remain equal at all times.

The requirements for election judges are that:

- They must be a registered voter.
- They must be of good character and be able to read and write.
- They must not hold a public office.
- They must sign a statement swearing to their honest intent.

No one whose relative is on the ballot can serve as an election judge. This can make recruiting judges a problem in small communities.

Usually a local party leader submits a list of eligible judges to the local election board, which picks the judges. Prior to election day, the judges are paid to attend courses that train them for their duties.

Above all, election judges are supposed to ensure the secrecy of each ballot. Once a voter begins to complete a ballot, judges are not supposed to see the ballot or hover nearby. But if a voter needs help once he or she in the voting booth, a judge may still help. As a safeguard

Voters line up outside the polls in Birmingham, Alabama.

against foul play, voters are likely to be helped by two officials of opposing parties, as required by most states' laws.

Voters who are blind, unable to read, or unable to mark a ballot can get help. It will come from two officials from different parties.

Poll Watchers   Poll watchers are representatives of a party or a candidate who sit at the polls to make sure the election process is conducted fairly. Not just any interested person may be a poll watcher. Like the election judges, they must be officially designated by a party or candidate, and they may have to be registered as an official watcher.

If a poll watcher witnesses any wrongdoing at the polls, he or she reports to the election judges or tells higher election authorities. If a poll watcher is caught electioneering, or causing a disruption in the polling place, he or she may be thrown out by by the election judges. The judges may even call the police for assistance.

The History of Balloting

In the early years of the United States secret paper ballots were not commonly used. Sometimes the colonists used the Native Americans' ancient "corn and bean" ballot system. In this system, a corn kernel dropped into the ballot box was a vote for one candidate and a bean dropped in the box was a vote for the other. More often, oral voting was used. In this method of voting, a voter stood before election officials and stated his vote out loud. Electioneers and often the candidates themselves were often there to slap the voter's back if he voted "correctly."

In the 1800s the use of paper ballots—informally called "papers" —gained popularity, but voting still was not carried out in secrecy. Each party printed its own ballot on colored paper that listed *only* the names of its own candidates. At the polls, in plain sight, electioneers hustled to supply voters with their party ballot. By watching to see what color of ballot a person accepted, it was easy to tell which way he was voting.

By the 1880s, a new balloting method had been introduced, based on the method used in Australia. It called for paper ballots to be printed at public expense and supplied directly to each voter by official election judges. The ballots listed the names of *all* candidates. Thus a voter could mark the ballot and turn

Portable voting booths are wheeled down a street in Cleveland in 1891 before an election. These early voting booths were lighted by oil lamps and heated by stoves that often burned the voters.

it in without letting anyone know whom he had voted for. Gradually all of the states began using this Australian ballot.

Types of Ballots Today

Today, most polling places use computer punch card ballots or voting machines. In the punch card system, a voter punches holes into a card which is fixed under a ballot. A computer later counts the votes by counting the holes. A voting machine may have a series of switches, one for each candidate on the ballot. The voter flips the switches to indicate his or her choices, and then pulls a lever to record the vote and clear the machine for the next voter.

Politicians know it can make a difference how the candidates are listed on the ballot. Some communities use the so-called **office block** ballot that lists the candidates under the title of the office they're pursuing. The office block is disliked by party leaders because it directs the voter's attention to the office, not the party, and discourages straight-ticket voting.

Party leaders prefer the **party column** ballot in which candidates are listed vertically under the name of the party. In about half of the states, it is possible to vote for a straight ticket of candidates from one party with a single stroke of the hand. The party column ballot is thought to encourage this process.

Some elections—such as community and school board races—are **non-partisan** elections. In these elections, no candidates are listed by party designation.

Write-in Votes

Election judges must, on request, show voters how to cast **write-in votes**. A write-in vote is a vote for someone whose name is not printed on the ballot. The voter can write in any name on the ballot. But a vote for Superman might not be counted. In many states, write-in candidates must have filed a declaration of intent before election day in order for votes in their favor to be counted. A write-in vote may not count if cast for just anybody.

Tallying the Votes

At seven o'clock in the evening, most of the nation's polls begin closing. This is when election night becomes something to watch.

At each precinct, election judges begin immediately to prepare the precinct's ballots for **tabulation**, or sorting and counting, so the totals can be assembled and reported for broadcast to the voters.

In precincts using paper ballots or voting machines, the results might be tallied on the spot or sent to a central location. The paper ballots may either be counted aloud or counted by an optical scanner, a machine that reads the ballots. Each voting machine shows its results on a meter.

In any case, the count is double-checked by an official of an opposing party in the presence of poll watchers before it is delivered to a regional bureau of the state board of election comissioners. Either the count is delivered by at least two poll officials of different parties, or the results are sealed and then delivered by an official transporter.

In precincts using punch cards, the cards are normally counted at a counting center by computer. In case of a breakdown, a backup computer facility is kept ready. The ballots are counted by trained employees of the election board or by a computer-company expert.

Absentee Ballots

If a voter is ill, disabled, out of town, or in the military at election time, he or she can still vote by filing an **absentee ballot**, either by mail or in person.

Voters may cast their ballots at their election board any time from a month or more before the election until sometime the day before the election, depending on the state.

Voters who send their ballots by mail must be sure their ballots are received by the close of the polls on election day.

Recounts and Runoffs

Even after election night, the results may not be official.

In 1977, Ruth Sims was elected Selectwoman of Greenwich, Connecticut, by six votes. In a recount, Republican opponent Rupert Vernon was awarded a one-vote lead. Sims then went to court claiming "irregularities" in the tallying of 545 absentee ballots. The court ordered a second recount that Sims won by one vote. But the election was not over yet. After more court hearings, the election was called a tie, and in a special runoff election, Sims was elected by a clear margin.

In 1974, Republican Louis Wyman defeated Democrat John Durkin by two votes in a race for a U.S. Congressional seat in New Hampshire. But Durkin went to the state senate with a petition to review the election results. After seven months of confusion the senate could not decide whether the election had been conducted properly or not. The seat was declared vacant and a special election was held. This time Durkin won handily.

Recounts of election results are not common, but they can happen. In some states a recount is required if the results of an election are of a certain closeness. Otherwise, a candidate or a voter may file a petition to request a recount. If there is reasonable evidence that a large number of votes were cast or counted improperly, especially if the number of questionable votes could change who won, the recount will be granted.

Often a recount leads to an order for a runoff election. Other times a winner is decided simply on the results of the recount. But the results of a recount don't always produce a "new" winner. In 1978, Lansing, Michigan, Councilman Jack Cunther won by two votes. In a recount he won again—this time by one vote, 2817 to 2816.

James K. Polk was elected president in 1844 in an election run on fraud. For example, one of Polk's supporters sent a boatload of Democrats up the Mississippi. The boat stopped at three spots so the men could vote at each place.

7

Stolen Votes

It was said to be a buyer's market for voters in St. Landry Parish, Louisiana, during the 1970s. If you lived in the right neighborhood, and agreed to vote as you were told, you could sell your vote for $2 and sometimes as much as $5. It was good money for poor families in the area.

Often voters got cash up front from a political worker who would come to their house and drive them to the polls. Other times voters would enter the polling place and ask for assistance from an election judge wearing a red shirt. If the voter allowed that judge to help him or her cast a vote "correctly," the judge would hand the voter a token to be turned in later for cash.

The tokens were used because the candidates wanted to make sure that the people they hired to pay the voters did not keep the money for themselves. In shady politics, people learn not to trust anyone.

Election fraud has been part of the American electoral process from the beginning. Sometimes the method is bribery, other times it is miscounting ballots, recruiting bogus votes, or simply threatening officials and voters with violence.

Vote Early and Often

In the early days of the country, the practice of registering voters had not yet begun. Even into the 1900s, some communities did not require

49

registration. The result was that hired voters could go from one precinct to the next, voting again and again. A pep talk given by party leaders to their troops became "Vote early and often."

Tombstone Votes and Other Tricks

More and more communities began to require registration as a way of cracking down on fraud. Crafty political thinkers found new ways to beat the system.

One tactic was the **tombstone vote** in which dead voters were kept on registration lists and ballots were cast in their names. Another ploy was establishing fake identities and residences for imaginary voters and having stand-ins cast fraudulent votes for these imaginary voters as well as for themselves.

At the turn of the century, fraud was especially blatant in Philadelphia, where the city was run by corrupt political leaders who controlled the whole voting process. In one election, an investigation discovered 250 votes cast in a ward with fewer than 100 registered voters. The registration list was found to be padded with names of dead and imaginary people. In another election, 80,000 of 204,000 votes cast

were found to be false. Philadelphia police—who were controlled by the corrupt politicians—had allowed people to vote repeatedly, arresting only those who dared to protest.

Fraud of this type has continued to take place in more modern times. In Georgia during the mid-1940s, for example, a special election was held to replace Governor Eugene Talmadge, who had died in office. His son, Herman, won the election, but it turned out that 32 votes for him were cast by the same man under 32 names. At least two of the alleged "voters" were dead; five had moved away; five said they had not even gone to the polls; and another dozen could not be found.

Voting fraud is illegal, of course. It is a felony, for example, for a noncitizen to vote. And in Louisiana today, bribing for votes carries a fine of between $500 and $1,000 and a prison term of not more than one year for anyone convicted.

But voting fraud historically has been hard to pin down, so fraud continues—especially when authorities can be paid to look the other way.

Confusing the Voters

In 1954, Mildred Younger defeated California State Senator Jack Tenney in a primary election, despite a clever trick pulled by Tenney's supporters. In an effort to confuse people who planned to vote for Younger, Tenney's backers persuaded another person named Younger to join the ballot in hopes that the Younger vote would be split between the two.

Confusing voters is a popular way of diluting an opponent's strength. The key is for one side to make absolutely sure they understand the plan. On election day, that side will not be confused by the trick, but their opponent's supporters might be fooled into wasting their votes.

For example, if a group that proposes to build a nuclear power plant must put the proposal to a popular vote, they might be worried about the outcome. If the proposal must win a majority of support, but many people oppose nuclear power and will probably vote against the proposal, some confusion might help.

With careful planning, the group should be able to ensure that the proposal is phrased in a complicated way on the ballot. A vote "Yes," for example, might actually mean "Yes, we do *not* want the power plant." A vote "No," might mean, "No, we do *not* want the proposal defeated."

If the group has organized a massive campaign and has fully briefed its supporters, they should turn out at the polls in large numbers and vote correctly. Meanwhile, the group can hope its opponents have not been fully educated. The result is that many opponents might unwittingly vote to support the power plant.

Through history there have been several other tricks used to confuse voters. One is the "bedsheet ballot" ploy, in which a group tries to get as many items as possible on the ballot to make it as long as a bedsheet. Many of the items may be virtually meaningless, but they will help confuse and frustrate many voters. They also hide the one or two important items buried in the ballot.

Other tricks are to establish more than one polling place in a precinct, or to switch the site of the polling place just before election day. Politicians who use these tricks will make sure their supporters know the official place to vote.

Intimidation

Killings on election day were fairly common during the mid-1800s. At the height of its influence, the Know-Nothing Party could be especially violent at election time.

In 1855, gangs of Know-Nothings

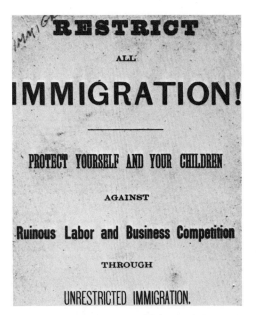

The anti-immigration poster above shows fear of immigrants which was widespread in the mid-1800s. German emigrants embarking for New York (above right) were only part of a huge wave of European immigrants.

in Louisville, Kentucky, beat, stabbed, and shot German and Irish immigrants preparing to vote. When angry immigrants killed several Know-Nothing supporters, Know-Nothings attacked German and Irish neighborhoods, burning homes, and shooting those who tried to escape. In all, 20 people were killed and Know-Nothing candidates won at the polls with hardly a German or Irish vote cast.

During the late 1800s, the Ku Klux Klan used violence in some parts of the South to influence the vote.

A Congressional investigation in 1868 found that three weeks before election day that year, 2,000 blacks had been killed or beaten in Louisiana, and the Ku Klux Klan was the prime suspect.

During the 1920s, Prohibition made alcoholic drinks illegal. Some gangs became rich selling liquor outside the law. In Chicago, Al Capone and other gangsters donated $300,000 to Republican Mayor William "Big Bill" Thompson's campaign. Early one election day in Chicago, two Democratic precinct offices were bombed, two election judges were beaten, and many voters were frightened from the polls by the threat of gang violence. Extra police cruised the city the rest of the day. The violence stopped, but few votes were cast against Thompson.

Gerrymandering

In 1983, Republican Governor George Deukmejian enraged California Democrats when he proposed to have the state's voting districts redefined. A voting district might include ten city blocks or thousands of square miles, but its boundaries are carefully defined. The California Democrats thought Deukmejian would have the boundaries moved to the advantage of Republican candidates. What Democrats feared was the possibility of **gerrymandering**, one of the oldest, trickiest ways of rigging elections.

Gerrymandering is the practice of drawing election district boundaries to include or exclude certain groups, either to strengthen or weaken their voting power. It takes its name after Massachusetts Governor Elbridge Gerry, one of the signers of the Declaration of Independence.

In 1812, Gerry redrew the boundaries of the voting districts in Massachusetts so his party could win more seats in the legislature. One of Gerry's districts took such a cockeyed shape that one legislator said it looked like a salamander.

"No," said another legislator. "You mean a Gerrymander."

Gerrymandering works like this: Voting-district boundary lines are set, for example, so that a district of 50,000 mostly Hispanic voters is awarded one representative, and six other districts of just 10,000 mostly white voters are each given one representative, too. Or the lines are drawn through the heart of the Hispanic neighborhoods to split them. The Hispanics then vote in districts where they are outnumbered by white voters. Instead of one Hispanic representative and five white representatives, the voters in a city combine to elect *no* Hispanic representatives and six white representatives. The effect is that the voting power of the Hispanics has been negated.

In Alabama in the late 1950s, black residents of Tuskegee, Alabama, charged the state with drawing the city's election districts in a way that diluted the black vote. They said what had once been a square-shaped district had been redrawn into an "irregular, 28-sided figure."

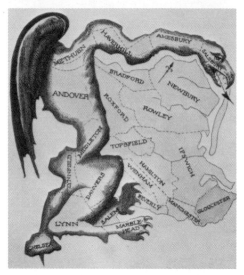

Elbridge Gerry (top) will long be remembered as the creator of the gerrymander (bottom). However, he also was a member of the Constitutional Convention and served as vice president under James Madison.

The state of Alabama claimed it had the right to fashion its political districts any way it wanted. But the Supreme Court rejected that claim in 1963, saying the federal government has the right to rule as to the fairness of how districts are drawn.

"Political equality...can mean only one thing—one person, one vote," Justice William O. Douglas said. If not, the judge said, a voter in Georgia's smallest district would have 99 times the voting influence of a voter in Atlanta.

Through the 1960s, all state legislatures were required to redraw their voting districts on the basis of one person, one vote. The effect was to equalize the number of people in each district no matter what the size of the district was geographically. This process of setting up districts for fair representation is called **reapportionment.**

Another recent measure that has cut the impact of gerrymandering is the switch in many communities to **at-large** elections. In these elections, a resident casts votes for a full slate of politicians who will serve the community as a whole, not just for a single official who will represent a single area. At-large elections help minorities, who may be numerous but concentrated in a single area of a community, by giving them representation in fair proportion to their numbers.

Abusing Absentee Ballots

Absentee ballots are fertile ground for vote fraud. Because voters may cast absentee ballots through the mail, and because voters can vote absentee any time from a month or more before the election until election day itself, it is difficult to supervise the process. There is plenty of room for voting misconduct.

A soldier stationed overseas has no way of knowing whether his or her absentee ballot is counted correctly.

For example, campaign workers often visit a senior citizens' home just before an election to help the residents cast their absentee ballots. It would be easy for campaign workers to offer extra "help" in filling out the ballots with a vote for the candidate they represent.

Absentee ballots sometimes have been the margin of victory, even in state-wide elections. In 1962, for example, Rhode Island Republican John Chafee won his first term as governor by 398 absentee ballots.

Miscounting the Count

When considering vote fraud, probably the first method that comes to mind is simply miscounting the votes that are cast. Election judges have been known to cheat, but computerization and strict supervision of the voting process have made this less common in recent years.

When the votes have been miscounted on purpose, the most common way to cheat has been by awarding some of the votes for third-party or write-in candidates to one of the stronger contenders. This method is considered less conspicuous than tampering with votes cast for one of the two major candidates.

Franklin D. Roosevelt supported the end of Prohibition. Voters for whom that was an important issue turned out to help Roosevelt win in 1932. These customers are celebrating the end of Prohibition in 1933 in Los Angeles.

8

Election Turnout

In 1976, Democrat Jimmy Carter was elected by only 27 percent of all Americans qualified to cast ballots. In 1980, 28 percent of those qualified to vote combined to elect Ronald Reagan. In fact, no president in history has been elected by a majority of the eligible voters and, from 1960 until 1984, each election turned out smaller and smaller percentages of the voting-age population.

Voter turnout is the number of eligible voters who actually vote in an election. In 1960, the race between John Kennedy and Richard Nixon drew an all-time high of 62.8 percent of the voting-age population to the polls. Then voter turnout in general elections decreased year after year

until 1984. That year the trend reversed when the Walter Mondale-

Gerald R. Ford greets a crowd during his 1976 campaign. Many of the eligible voters stayed home on election day.

Ronald Reagan contest attracted 53.6 percent to the polls—an increase of about a percentage point from 1980.

The decreasing turnout is explained in large part by the fact that some groups have felt cut out of politics for the past couple of decades. Blacks, women, poor people, young people as well as the elderly, environmentalists, and gays were among those who felt their votes did not really matter. The voting upswing in 1984 may reflect the renewed confidence of these groups in the election process.

Who Votes? Who Doesn't?

Women and Men   After women were awarded the right to vote in 1920, they consistently voted in lower proportions than men did. But in 1980, the percentage of eligible women voters who cast ballots was equal to the percentage of eligible men voters who cast ballots. In 1984, the turnout of eligible women voters was nearly two points higher than men voters, 60.8 to 59.0. And because women outnumber men, women cast 53.3 percent of the votes that year—more than seven million more votes than men.

Blacks and Whites   Black voter turnout leaped from 50.5 percent of the eligible population in 1980 to 55.8 percent in 1984. The successful candidacy of Jesse Jackson, a black man who won two Democratic primaries and earned 10 percent of the vote in several others, is a prime reason. Jackson's candidacy proved even more successful in 1988, drawing an even larger percentage of blacks to the polls.

As a matter of comparison, 59.2 percent of the eligible white voters participated in 1980, rising to 59.9 in 1984. White Americans have generally enjoyed more privileges than black Americans—such as better chances for good jobs and good schooling. And their higher voter turnout might show that whites are more likely to believe that voting does some good in their lives.

The Poor   Studies from the 1984 election show that poor people are less likely to vote than those with more money. In 1984, among people with an annual income of $5,000 or less, only 39 percent of the voting-age population turned out. In contrast, about 75 percent of the voting-age population making $25,000 a year or more cast a vote that year.

Poor people are likely to feel that their needs are not being met by the government. Many do not vote because they believe their votes make no difference.

Young People   Results from 1984 show that 44.7 percent of the nation's 18-to-20-year-olds were registered to vote and that 35.7 percent actually cast a ballot that year. The figures are roughly equal to those young voters posted in the three previous elections.

Like many blacks and poor people, many young adults may not vote because they do not believe their votes make any impact. Many young people have low-paying jobs and little money and may feel powerless compared to older, established adults. Also, they may not see any impact of politics on their own lives.

Single-issue Voters   High voter turnout in any election may often be explained by the participation of **single-issue voters.** These are people inspired to vote almost solely on the basis of their feelings on a certain issue such as abortion, busing, school prayer, or the environment. They vote to make sure the candidate who supports their position is elected—or to make sure the candidate whose position they disagree with is defeated.

Single-issue voters might care most strongly about the Vietnam War (as these protesters did), or about abortion, or handgun control, or almost anything else.

The changing issues that have motivated single-issue voters virtually tell the story of America: westward expansion of the country in the 1840s, the abolition or the spread of slavery in the 1860s, Prohibition in the 1920s, women's rights in the 1980s.

When organized behind an emotional issue of the day, single-issue voters can account for a large portion of the election turnout.

Turnout by State   In 1984, the

state with the highest percentage turnout of its voting age population was Minnesota, where 68.5 percent of the voters voted. The candidacy of Minnesotan Walter Mondale for president helps explain why so many Minnesotans turned out. The same year, South Carolina had the lowest turnout of its voting age population, only 40.2 percent.

Turnout by Country In Australia, voting is a duty. Voters are fined if they do not vote and lack a good excuse. As a result, turnout there is always more than 95 percent. Critics say the system simply forces uninformed people to vote.

Even without the requirement to vote, however, many other countries have higher voter participation than the United States. When voter turnout of countries whose governments and economies are similar to the United States' are compared with voter turnout in the United States, the U.S. falls at the bottom of the list.

What Affects Turnout

The process of registering to vote is sometimes blamed for poor voter turnout in America. In the United States, voters must come forward to register. Voters must supply the documents to prove they are who they say they are, they live in the voting district, and they are eligible to vote. The process may prevent fraudulent votes, but it also keeps some eligible voters away from the polls because it is inconvenient and it is entirely the voter's responsibility. In Canada and some other democracies, the government bears the burden of making sure voters are registered properly. Some studies show that those who become registered are more than 70 percent likely to vote in the next election.

Voter turnout in America is lower in off-year elections. Voters are not as interested when presidential candidates are not on the ballot. Also, the weather—good or bad—can alter the turnout. When weather is bad, fewer older people may show up at the polls, for example, which can hurt a candidate who might be counting on their support. Other candidates might celebrate bad weather, because it might keep unsympathetic older voters away from the polls.

9
Getting Out the Vote

In 1981, the city of San Diego voted by mail on whether to build a convention center. Ballots were mailed to registered voters. The voters filled them out, signed them, and mailed them back. Each signature was then verified against each voter's registration form. One result of this election-by-mail was the defeat of the convention center proposal.

Another result was record-high voter participation for the city. A third result was the saving of an estimated $200,000 in election costs. At least for one election, San Diego found a solution to a problem that has nagged politicians and social activists for years: how to get people to vote.

For politicians, winning a person's agreement is one thing, and getting that person to the polls to actually cast a ballot is another. Politicians

In the 1960s, volunteers explain the voting machine to potential voters.

must actively encourage voters to go to the polls. This is particularly important in close local races, in which voters tend to vote along long-established party lines. Party loyalty leaves relatively few voters on the fence, so it is vital for each politician to make sure his or her people get out and vote.

On election day, politicians use fleets of volunteers to get people to the polls. The volunteers make last-minute telephone calls to remind people to vote, give rides to the polls, and serve as babysitters for voters with small children.

Often a massive, organized effort can pay off well. When Harold Washington, a black man, ran for mayor of Chicago in 1983, for example, his campaign drew an enormous black voter turnout. In fact, 90 percent of blacks ages 18 to 25 turned out. Normally only 10 percent of that group had gone to the polls. The black voters' support was the deciding factor in Washington's victory.

Party Bosses and Machines

From the late 1800s until well into the middle of this century, many big cities were "owned" by bosses of **political machines**. There was Tammany Hall in New York City during the late 1800s and early 1900s, run for years by Boss William Tweed. Later there was Boss Crump in Memphis, Mayor Hague in Jersey City, and Mayor Richard Daley in Chicago, among many other bosses in other cities.

The machines treated the city governments as their own private companies. Their supporters got the city jobs, such as garbage collector or police officer. If the city was considering building a public housing project, a supporter of the machine would be hired to build it. Wherever money moved in the city government, some money stuck to the men who ran the machine. They struck deals and schemes on behalf of the city machine without the public's knowledge. They used bribes and threats to avoid being held accountable for their illegal activities.

Probably no other American institution was more effective in getting its backers to the polls than the political machines.

The machines kept their supporters loyal because they also served a benevolent role as their city's welfare system. Long before welfare even existed, the machines provided groceries for the hungry, jobs for the unemployed, and housing for the homeless. They took care of people's

A cartoon about the Tammany Hall political machine. The caption read, "Who stole the people's money?—Do tell. 'Twas him.'"

basic needs without asking embarrassing questions. If a person had a problem, he or she could get help from the neighborhood precinct captain, who was one of the city boss's men. All of this help could be had for one price—a vote on election day.

A Single Vote Counts

In a country of more than 240 million people, one American's vote might seem meaningless. Actually, one vote means more than some people think.

People who do not vote might believe their absence is viewed as a defiant protest. More likely it is simply ignored. Even when thousands or millions of people dislike a candidate, if they do not vote against the candidate, they do not count. Their absence from the polls might let a candidate win by a large margin. He or she may then claim a "mandate" and govern with confidence because of his or her "decisive" victory.

In some communities, the number of votes cast in the last general election determines how many delegates the community can send to the next national party convention. So just turning out to vote can be important, no matter who the vote is for.

Adolph Hitler was elected the leader of the Nazi Party in 1932 by a single vote.

Some American elections have also been close.

In 1960, John Kennedy defeated Richard Nixon in the race for president by an average of less than one vote per precinct. Kennedy carried Illinois by only 8,858 votes out of 4,757,409 cast. A change of fewer than 9,000 votes in Illinois and Missouri would have denied him a majority of electoral votes nationwide.

Figured another way, if 15,000 of the approximately 69 million people who voted across the country had cast their ballots for Nixon instead of Kennedy in four key states—Hawaii, South Carolina, Illinois, and Missouri—Nixon would have won the election.

In 1976, a shift of 3,687 votes in Hawaii and 5,559 in Ohio would have allowed Gerald Ford to defeat Jimmy Carter.

In 1964, U.S. Senator Howard Cannon of Nevada was re-elected by 48 votes.

In 1962, a state representative to the Connecticut General Assembly was elected by one vote: 4,164 to 4,163.

In 1981, Chon Guitierrez and Stanley Langland tied for a seat on the school board in Belmont, California, and drew straws to determine the winner.

10
The Right to Vote

In the summer of 1963, in the city of Greenwood, Mississippi, nine college students tried to lead 200 black residents to the city courthouse to register them to vote. The students were arrested.

The students, all members of the Student Nonviolent Coordinating Committee, were charged with disturbing the peace. They were denied permission to call an attorney and were put to trial on the spot. They each were assessed fines of $200 and sentenced to 120 days hard labor at a county farm.

At the farm they were abused by guards and, in protest, refused to work or eat. As punishment they were transferred to the state penitentiary. There they were put in solitary confinement and at least one student was hung by his hands for several hours from the cell bars.

Jesse Jackson worked with the Southern Christian Leadership Conference in the 1960s and is still active in civil rights.

On August 28, 1963, more than 250,000 demonstrators came to Washington, D.C., to show that they wanted government to act to guarantee blacks fair treatment and equal opportunities—including voting rights.

After 55 days the students were finally bailed out. They were told they would be shot if they ever returned to Greenwood.

For blacks, and many other groups, securing the right to vote in the United States has been far from easy. Several key **civil rights** acts were passed in the 1960s to strike down practices that for years had denied people their chance to vote. Even so, as recently as 1983, black leader

Jesse Jackson unearthed continued efforts to keep minority people from voting.

In 1983, Jackson invited William Reynolds, the head of the Civil Rights Division of the Justice Department, to tour Mississippi. Jackson offered Reynolds an up-close look at cases of registration centers that closed whenever election officials decided to close them, companies that would not let blacks leave their jobs to register, polling places that were moved without notice, and black voters sent away from the polls by imposters pretending to be election officials. Reynolds sent federal officials to five Mississippi counties to clean up the abuse.

By contrast, in early America, the federal government was part of the problem in denying people an opportunity to vote. In fact, our voting rights have developed slowly. The process has sometimes been ugly, but for the most part it has been successful.

The Fear of Common People

Before America won independence from England, Jews and Roman Catholics were not allowed to vote in most colonies. In other American communities, Quakers and Baptists had no vote. Jews, in fact, did not gain full, nationwide voting rights until 1842.

During the colonial period, the educated landowners were afraid to allow working-class people and those with "different" beliefs or backgrounds to vote. Much of their fear was based on prejudice. They truly believed their wealth, property, education, ancestry, and religion made them better than others. Some of their fear came from the belief that these "lower" classes would use their vote to rise to power. If the Roman Catholics, for example, controlled the government, they would surely make it illegal to practice any religion but theirs. And if debtors had power, they would surely do something frightful like declaring all debts off—without repaying them.

When the colonies became a nation, all of the original 13 states limited voting rights to adult white male property holders and taxpayers. Seven states required land ownership, but the other six defined owners of cattle or machinery as "property" holders, too. The result was that even among adult white men, fewer than half were allowed to vote. In the elections of 1780, for example, only about 120,000 out of a population of two million were eligible to vote.

In the early 1800s, working-class people had an influential supporter in Thomas Jefferson. In the early 1820s, Andrew Jackson was on their side. Both Jefferson and Jackson worked to advance the voting rights of common people, partly because both men knew that working-class votes were likely to be cast in their favor.

Gradually, the seven states requiring land ownership reduced the requirement to taxpaying. By the mid-1800s, voters did not even have to be taxpayers in many places, although some states hung on to the requirement into the 20th century. Of course, women, youths, blacks, and Native Americans were still out of luck.

Abraham Lincoln's Emancipation Proclamation declared "all persons held as Slaves" within the rebellious states of the South to be "FOREVER FREE."

Blacks and the Vote

The fall of the property-owning and taxpaying requirements was only the first step for many Americans in obtaining the right to vote. Blacks were not specifically given the right to vote until after the Civil War.

When they were owned as slaves, black people were considered property. They could not vote any more than a bull could vote. The Emancipation Proclamation of January 1, 1863, guaranteed freedom to slaves in Confederate states, and the 13th Amendment to the Constitution ended slavery in the whole country in 1865. Blacks still were not considered full citizens, however, and could not vote. The 14th Amendment to the Constitution was ratified in 1868, awarding citizenship to former slaves. It still took the 15th Amendment, ratified in 1870, to prohibit any state from denying the vote to anyone on account of "race, color or previous condition of servitude."

State lawmakers, especially in the South, immediately went to work coming up with a string of laws designed to keep blacks from voting. The laws did not discriminate because of race—they did not mention race at all—so they were not technically unconstitutional. But their purpose was clearly to keep blacks from the polls.

Grandfathers, Taxes, and Reading Tests

Blacks were refused ballots for several reasons:

- Because they didn't have a grandfather who voted.
- Because they hadn't paid a **poll tax**, carefully set too high for most newly freed slaves to be able to afford.
- Because they couldn't pass a reading test, a test that was given only to blacks.
- Because they were not able to "properly" interpret the Constitution.
- Because their character was not considered "good enough."
- Because they hadn't voted in a primary election that they were not allowed to vote in anyway.

In 1915 the United States Supreme Court found the "grandfather" clause unconstitutional.

In 1964 the 24th Amendment to the Constitution outlawed the poll tax in federal elections. They were still used in state elections, however, until an act of Congress and a Supreme Court decision made all poll taxes illegal.

The **literacy** or reading test was not given to anyone who was a voter in 1867 or a descendent of someone who voted that year. The blacks were not given the right to vote until 1870. Because no blacks could meet the literacy test requirements, they were forced to take the test even when many illiterate whites did not. Blacks almost uniformly could not pass the test because it had been a crime to teach slaves to read and any slave who *could* read could have been punished for the "crime."

There is a story of a black doctor of philosophy who was required by an election officer to read an American newspaper, followed by a French newspaper, and a German newspaper. He read each of them perfectly and was able to translate the French and German into English. The scholar then was handed a Chinese paper, which he could not decipher. The officer declared, "I guess you can't read."

Congress attacked the literacy tests with the Civil Rights Acts of 1957 and 1960 and the Voting Rights Act of 1965. Although they are not strictly unconstitutional even today, literacy tests now must be "fairly administered" and may not be used with the intent of denying any group's right to vote. Further, in 1970, Congress suspended all literacy

Blacks wait in line to register for the vote in Brooklyn, New York, in the 1960s. Volunteers from organizations such as the National Association for the Advancement of Colored People (N.A.A.C.P.) have made a difference by helping people register and offering information about voting.

tests for a period of five years and they have not resurfaced since then.

Tests of whether one could "understand" or "properly interpret" the Constitution and tests of "good character" also were administered as a way of screening out unwanted voters.

As might be expected, the Constitution tests were made so difficult that a Supreme Court justice would have had trouble passing them. In any case, the official who judged whether the interpretation was "proper" had the final say. The rules for scoring the good character tests could be made up on the spot.

One other method of voter discrimination was the "white" primary. Only whites could vote in these primaries, which selected party nominees. How could this be legal? State officials claimed that political parties were "private organizations" and that the Constitution applied only to actions of the states. The officials claimed that the 15th Amendment—which forbids citizens to be denied the right to vote—did not apply to primaries because primaries are not state elections, only meetings held by private organizations.

In 1944, the U.S. Supreme Court struck down white primaries. It said that primary elections *are* protected by the 15th Amendment because political parties are acting as state agencies when they are carrying out the election process.

Congress passed several bills in the 1960s to rid the country of voting injustice. The 1964 Civil Rights Act, in addition to abolishing poll taxes, forbade the use of different voting requirements for whites and minorities. The 1965 Voting Rights Act authorized federal election officials to take control of any election district found to be discriminating in the voting process.

Once these laws were passed, many young people from around the country volunteered to go South in buses to help blacks register to vote. Sometimes the volunteers met with violence. Some were beaten or shot and others were jailed. Many blacks were beaten or arrested when they tried to register. But federal voting legislation eventually had a major impact in the South. Before the 1965 act was passed, only 35,000 blacks had been registered in all of Mississippi. After it passed the number climbed to 200,000. By 1967 Mississippi had elected 22 blacks to public office.

Others Who Struggled

Black Americans are not the only group whose right to vote was a long time coming. American Indians had been denied the right to vote from the founding of the United States until they finally were granted full citizenship in 1953. In 1924 they had been put on hold when Congress had granted them "qualified" rather than full citizenship. This "qualified" status allowed many states to deny Native Americans the right to vote.

As for women, they were not allowed to vote in any of the original 13 states, although there was no federal law that forbade them that right. Some states and territories, such as Wyoming, freely allowed women to vote in state and local elections. In fact, the first woman in Congress, Representative Jeannette Rankin of Montana, first served from 1917 to 1919. She could vote on bills in Congress before she could vote in a national election. It took a formal fight of 72 years to

Above: A suffrage parade in 1912. Below right: Women were allowed to vote in some local elections, such as this primary in 1908, before the 19th Amendment was ratified.

win the right to vote nationally. The fight began in 1848, when Elizabeth Cady Stanton issued a call for a Women's Rights Convention to be held at Seneca Falls, New York. This was recognized as the first public demand for female suffrage. Seventy-two years later, well after Stanton's death, the fight was won. The 19th Amendment to the Constitution, passed in 1920, meant that women finally could vote for president.

During the 1960s, the Vietnam War was a boiling national issue. Young people were frustrated because they were old enough to be drafted into the armed forces at 18,

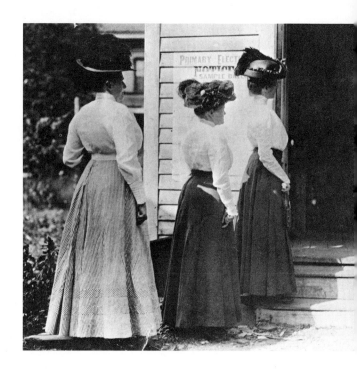

but were not allowed to vote until age 21. They began a movement to lower the voting age.

Georgia Governor Ellis Arnall had first advanced the idea during World War II that a person should be old enough to vote if he were old enough to be a soldier. In fact, in Arnall's state, as well as in Kentucky, Alaska, and Hawaii, 18-year-old residents were allowed to vote before the rest of the country caught up. In 1971, the 26th Amendment finally was ratified. It said that the states and federal government could not deny 18-year-olds the right to vote.

The same tactics that were used against blacks also have been used to deny other groups the right to vote. For example, the literacy tests were a handy way to exclude many groups. Congress's suspension of the literacy tests finally came about shortly after a case in 1970, involving Genoveva Castro, a native-born American woman of Mexican descent. She was not allowed to register to vote in California because of a clause in the state constitution that stated, "No person who shall not be able to read the constitution in English...shall ever exercise the privileges on an elector in this state."

Castro could read the constitution in Spanish. She sued the state claiming she was denied "equal protection under the law," which is guaranteed by the 14th Amendment. The state supreme court ruled in favor of Castro. This was a victory for countless Mexican-Americans and other non-English speaking Californians who had been kept from voting by that clause.

One sign at this suffragists' booth in 1912 says: "Women LEAVE the HOME to MARKET. They COULD VOTE on the way." Many men feared that if women left their "natural place" in the home they would become wild and unfeminine.

Republican candidate Alf Landon (above) launched his campaign with a showy parade in Newark, New Jersey, in 1936. The Literary Digest's poll was only one which picked Landon over Franklin D. Roosevelt (right). But even the Gallup poll, which predicted Roosevelt would win with 389 electoral votes to Landon's 141, was wrong. Roosevelt won 523 electoral votes—Landon had 8.

11
Polls and Predictions

In 1936, a popular magazine called *Literary Digest* picked Republican Governor Alf Landon to defeat Franklin Roosevelt and become the next president. The magazine was so sure of its prediction that future issues, printed before the election, referred to "President Landon."

On election night, Roosevelt crushed Landon at the polls, carrying every state except Maine and Vermont. Landon was unable even to win in Kansas, his home state.

What went wrong?

The big mistake *Literary Digest* made was in their **poll**. A poll is a careful study of how people feel about a certain topic. A **pollster** asks a small group of people questions, then predicts how the general public

would answer the questions based on the answers of the small group.

The magazine had asked their questions of people chosen from a list of automobile and telephone owners. Many people owned cars and phones in 1936, but many others did not. The magazine's "sample audience," therefore, did not represent voters from all walks of life.

It is true that among car and phone owners, people voted for Landon by 56 percent. But the nation as a whole chose Roosevelt.

In succeeding elections, the 1936 fiasco made pollsters cautious in their predictions. They continued to make mistakes, but their methods became much more reliable. Most polls today are accurate within three or four points of the percentage they predict.

How Polls Work

Most polling organizations ask their questions of about 1,500 people selected at random throughout the country. The opinions of only 1,500 people can reflect the opinions of more than 240 million Americans fairly accurately. The key is in the probabilities: if every person in the country has an equal chance of being selected in the sample of 1,500, then the sample should accurately represent the country as a whole. For each person selected, there are millions of others not selected who would say the same things if asked. The important element is that the sample is chosen at random.

Today, random samples are sometimes chosen from lists of telephone owners—exactly the practice that ruined the *Literary Digest* poll in 1936. But in modern times, almost all voters have a phone.

Uses of Polls

All presidential candidates and many candidates for lesser offices have their own private pollsters. The candidates use private polls not only to predict victory or defeat but to help find weaknesses in a candidate's campaign. The information can be used by a candidate to plot campaign strategy.

"Is there anything you don't like about candidate Jones?" a poll might ask. If people say they perceive him or her as "too rich," Jones might make a point of being seen digging ditches. If the poll sample says he or she is "too intellectual," the candidate might make sure to show up on television playing softball.

Polls are taken continually during a campaign, usually once every two weeks, so candidates can keep a close watch on the mood of the nation.

Why Polls Call It Wrong

One of the first polls taken in a U.S. presidential campaign was 100 percent correct although it failed to accurately predict the winner. In 1824 the *Pennsylvania*, a newspaper in Harrisburg, Pennsylvania, conducted a poll. It announced that Andrew Jackson would be the popular choice over John Quincy Adams that year. In fact, Jackson was the popular champion, but the election was decided in the House of Representatives. There, Adams was the eventual winner.

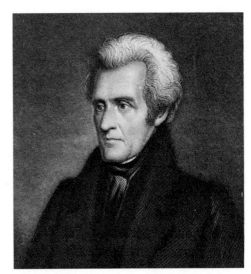

In 1824, a poll predicted that John Quincy Adams (left) would lose to Andrew Jackson (right). Adams became president, but the polls had predicted the vote correctly—the election was decided in the House of Representatives.

For any number of reasons, political polls can be in error:

- People's opinions are volatile. They may change their minds unexpectedly.
- Polls must take into account undecided voters, who can tip the balance of opinion when they finally make up their minds.
- People feel obligated to give an answer to pollsters. They may express an opinion even though they don't feel strongly about it.
- Many people will agree to take part in a poll, but it is difficult to predict who will actually go out and vote on election day.

A Problem with Polls

One major issue about the use of polls has nothing to do with how they are taken. Many people are concerned that they create a "self-fulfilling prophecy." They fear that if voters hear Candidate X is going to win, they might ask themselves "Why should I bother to vote? It's already settled." Further, if undecided voters hear Candidate Y is going to win, they might cast their votes for Candidate Y just to be on the side of the winner. In this way, polls may actually change the outcome of an election.

77

In 1976, President Gerald Ford (third from left) watched the election returns with his family and his running mate, Senator Robert Dole (third from right). Ford and Dole conceded the election that night, when the returns showed Carter had won 272 electoral votes—two more than needed to win.

12
The Early Call of the Winner

A black-and-white sketch from 1896 shows a dark, crowded street and people gazing up at a slide projection on the side of a building. The slide says "Boston Herald Bulletin: McKinley elected".

It was the first announcement in Boston that William McKinley had become president by defeating William Jennings Bryan.

In modern times, of course, election reports have become more sophisticated. Television in particular provides speedier coverage than was possible before its invention. In national elections this can be especially apparent.

In 1980, NBC called Ronald Reagan a winner in Ohio just a few minutes after polls closed in that state. By 8:15 P.M. East Coast time, the network had called Reagan the winner of the whole election.

Out in California it was still 5:15, with more than an one and a half hours left to vote. It was an hour earlier in Alaska, and the middle of the afternoon—3:15—in Hawaii. Yet CBS and ABC soon followed with their projections that Reagan was the winner.

Reagan did win by a huge electoral margin, proving all three networks right. But many people believed that was not the point. As they had in 1964 when Lyndon Johnson had won, and in 1972 when Richard Nixon was the winner, the networks all had reported a presidential victor before the polls closed in the western

Richard Nixon flashes the victory sign to his supporters in 1968. He was elected by only 43.3 percent of the popular vote in 1968, or about a fourth of all Americans of voting age.

part of the country. Was it fair, people asked, that a winner be declared so early, before everyone had had a chance cast a ballot?

Effects of the "Early Call"

In 1980, Jimmy Carter conceded at an unusually early hour, 8:30 P.M. Eastern time. Many West Coast Democrats were angry, not for what Carter's announcement might have done to his own chances, but for what it might have done to the chances of other Democrats. Who knows how many people might have gone out to vote—not only for president, but for other offices—but were discouraged by Carter's early withdrawal?

Political scientists who have studied the matter say it is difficult to know what effect an early call or an early concession has on voting. Asking people if it affects their voting behavior is unreliable, because people cannot comment unbiasedly on their own actions. Sketchy evidence suggests that some people might be discouraged from voting once a winner is announced. However, those who do vote after such an announcement are not likely to change the way they vote because of the news.

How Projections Are Made

Networks project who the winner will be on the basis of **exit polls**. These polls are taken in what researchers believe are "key" precincts. The pattern of the results in key precincts gives the experts enough information to pick a winner.

Exit polls are conducted during election day, usually by college students, who ask people how they voted as they emerge from the polling place. The exit poll ballots

Surrounded by family and supporters, a sad Hubert Humphrey concedes the victory to Nixon in 1968.

are put into a sealed box to be tallied later. The results are called in to a central office.

Normally about 12,000 to 15,000 subjects are interviewed in an exit poll. Some researchers say this makes it more reliable than the 1,500 normally used in a survey. But errors are still possible in the taking of any poll. Sometimes the networks incorrectly predict a senatorial or congressional race or how a state's electoral votes will go.

No pollster is ever certain whether the people answered the questions truthfully.

Why Make an Early Call

Networks project winners early for two basic reasons. The first is ratings. Being first with important news is believed to attract viewers. In the race to beat the competition, networks don't mind going out on a limb to be first with news, even if the news is unofficial.

The second is a duty to inform.

A joyous crowd celebrates Franklin D. Roosevelt's reelection in New York's Times Square in 1936.

News organizations have some obligation not to sit on what they know. If they are aware through their expert formulas that a certain candidate is bound to win, they feel the public has a right to know immediately.

Further, the networks believe they have used projections responsibly. They point out that in 1976 the race between Jimmy Carter and President Gerald Ford was too close to call until the early hours after election day, and no network made a hasty projection.

The Public Protest

In May 1981, 32 national organizations sent letters to all radio and television networks. They asked them to voluntarily stop making projections on election night before all the nation's polls had closed. The 32 groups hoped that asking for voluntary cooperation would save a long fight for legislation to accomplish the same goal.

The television and radio networks agreed with the groups not to make projections based on exit polls before all polling places closed. But they did not agree to stop making early projections on any other basis.

After the 1984 elections, the Committee for the Study of American Elections reported that the networks had not kept their word. They had made projections despite the agreement.

13
The Aftermath

"Someone asked me, as I came in, down on the street, how I felt," Adlai Stevenson said. He was speaking to his campaign workers in Illinois on election night 1952 after having been defeated for the presidency by Republican Dwight Eisenhower. "I was reminded of a story that a fellow townsman of ours used to tell—Abraham Lincoln. They asked him how he felt after an unsuccessful election. He said he felt like a boy who had stubbed his toe in the dark. He said that he was too old to cry but it hurt too much to laugh."

Stevenson must have felt the same way—or worse—four years later. In 1956 he ran again and lost again to the same man, Eisenhower. That election ended the dreams of another presidential hopeful, Estes Kefauver of Tennessee.

While in high school, Kefauver had written in a classmate's yearbook that his ambition was to be president. He started by running successfully for the U.S. House of Representatives. Next he was elected senator of Tennessee. When he ran for the Democratic presidential nomination in 1952 and 1956, however, he was defeated both times by Stevenson. And as Stevenson's vice presidential running mate in 1956, he was handed yet another defeat. Kefauver continued in politics, but he did not surface as a serious presidential contender again.

American history is littered with

names of candidates who were powerful people in their time, but who are not well known now because they never rose to the presidency. People like William Jennings Bryan, Henry Clay, and Thomas Dewey are only vaguely remembered today.

The Comebacks

Losing a presidential campaign does not have to be the end of a presidential quest. In 1888, for example, Democrat Grover Cleveland was defeated by Republican Benjamin Harrison. Cleveland came back to defeat Harrison in 1892.

And Richard Nixon's loss to John Kennedy in 1960 was only the beginning of a remarkable comeback. In the 1960 race, Nixon had the advantage of being the current vice president, under the popular Dwight Eisenhower, but he still lost. Two years later, he lost a race for governor in California, making his political career look all but over.

"You won't have Nixon to kick around anymore," Nixon told the news media at the time.

But Nixon came back. Eight years after losing to Kennedy, Nixon became president in a close victory over Democrat Hubert Humphrey and American Independent candidate George Wallace. And in 1972, he ran for reelection and won a resounding victory over Democrat George McGovern.

The Costs

In 1966, well-known millionaire Nelson Rockefeller spent more than $5 million of his own money to be elected to what at the time was a $50,000-a-year job—the governor of New York.

In a way, however, Rockefeller was fortunate. Many candidates spend heavily on campaigns only to lose the election. In the 1986 races for the U.S. Senate, for example, 8 of the top 15 spenders lost. Although Republican candidates raised more money than Democrats nationwide that year, the Republicans lost their majority in the Senate.

Similarly, in 1982, Mark Dayton spent $7.2 million, much of it his own money, in a U.S. Senate race in Minnesota. He lost to incumbent David Durenberger who spent less than $4 million.

Overall in the 1982 Senate races, candidates spent about $2 million apiece. Candidates for the House of Representatives spent about $200,000 each.

And the costs are always rising.

Radio and television advertising time, producing the ads, and the polls, research, and consultants behind them all cost more and seem more important every election.

The Winners

In 1828, Andrew Jackson, who was called a champion of the common man, was elected president. All of America was invited to attend the inauguration. Thousands came, and the crowd swelled beyond what the White House reception room could hold. Common folks mingled at the party with the upper-class people. Soon there were incidents of shoving, fighting, torn clothing, and broken furniture. No one was turned away, but the mob was finally coaxed outside the White House and punch was served on the front lawn for about 20,000 people.

Since Jackson's time, victors have won the office titles, the glory, and also the best parties. On election night, nearly every candidate for nearly every office will gather with his or her supporters to wait for the returns on television. Usually there is food, music, and, of course, hope for victory. Sometimes the vigil lasts long into the night, but when the losing opponent concedes his defeat

After the election, the work begins. President Kennedy at his desk in the White House.

with a short speech the election is over. It is left to the winners to enjoy the party, and then get to work.

For Further Reading

Butwin, Miriam, and Pat Pirmantgen. *Protest I: Boston Tea Party, Abolition, Women's Rights, and the Labor Movement.* Minneapolis, Minnesota: Lerner Publications, 1972.

Coolidge, Olivia. *Women's Rights: The Suffrage Movement in America, 1848-1920.* New York: E. P. Dutton & Co., Inc., 1966.

Corbin, Carole Lynn. *The Right to Vote.* New York: Franklin Watts, 1985.

King, Martin Luther. *Why We Can't Wait.* New York: Harper, 1958.

Kronenwetter, Michael. *The Threat from Within: Unethical Politics and Politicians.* New York: Franklin Watts, 1986.

O'Donnell, James J. *Every Vote Counts: A Teen-age Guide to the Electoral Process.* New York: Messner, 1976.

Williams, Juan. *Eyes on the Prize: America's Civil Rights Years, 1954-1965.* New York: Viking Penguin Inc., 1987.

Important Words

The terms listed below are defined on the indicated page:

Index